This Movie LogBook
Belongs to

MY MOVIE LOGBOOK

Movie Title

Director

Genre

Setting (Time & Place)

Main Cast

Supporting Cast

Plot

MY MOVIE LOGBOOK

My Review

Extra Notes

Rating: ☆☆☆☆☆

MY MOVIE LOGBOOK

Movie Title

Director

Genre

Setting (Time & Place)

Main Cast

Supporting Cast

Plot

MY MOVIE LOGBOOK

My Review

_____

_____

_____

_____

_____

_____

_____

_____

_____

_____

_____

_____

Extra Notes

_____

_____

_____

_____

Rating: ☆ ☆ ☆ ☆ ☆

MY MOVIE LOGBOOK

Movie Title

Director

Genre

Setting (Time & Place)

Main Cast

Supporting Cast

Plot

MY MOVIE LOGBOOK

My Review

_____

_____

_____

_____

_____

_____

_____

_____

_____

_____

_____

Extra Notes

_____

_____

_____

Rating: ☆☆☆☆☆

MY MOVIE LOGBOOK

Movie Title
_____

Director
_____

Genre
_____

Setting (Time & Place)
_____

_____

Main Cast
_____

_____

_____

Supporting Cast
_____

_____

Plot
_____

_____

_____

_____

_____

_____

_____

MY MOVIE LOGBOOK

My Review

_____

_____

_____

_____

_____

_____

_____

_____

_____

_____

Extra Notes

_____

_____

_____

Rating: ☆☆☆☆☆

MY MOVIE LOGBOOK

Movie Title
_____

Director
_____

Genre
_____

Setting (Time & Place)
_____

_____

Main Cast
_____

_____

_____

Supporting Cast
_____

_____

Plot
_____

_____

_____

_____

_____

_____

_____

MY MOVIE LOGBOOK

My Review

Extra Notes

Rating: ☆☆☆☆☆

MY MOVIE LOGBOOK

Movie Title

Director

Genre

Setting (Time & Place)

Main Cast

Supporting Cast

Plot

MY MOVIE LOGBOOK

My Review

_____

_____

_____

_____

_____

_____

_____

_____

_____

_____

_____

Extra Notes

_____

_____

_____

_____

Rating: ☆☆☆☆☆

MY MOVIE LOGBOOK

Movie Title

Director

Genre

Setting (Time & Place)

Main Cast

Supporting Cast

Plot

MY MOVIE LOGBOOK

My Review

Extra Notes

Rating: ☆☆☆☆☆

MY MOVIE LOGBOOK

Movie Title

Director

Genre

Setting (Time & Place)

Main Cast

Supporting Cast

Plot

MY MOVIE LOGBOOK

My Review

_____

_____

_____

_____

_____

_____

_____

_____

_____

_____

Extra Notes

_____

_____

_____

Rating: ☆☆☆☆☆

MY MOVIE LOGBOOK

Movie Title

Director

Genre

Setting (Time & Place)

Main Cast

Supporting Cast

Plot

MY MOVIE LOGBOOK

My Review

Extra Notes

Rating: ☆☆☆☆☆

MY MOVIE LOGBOOK

Movie Title

Director

Genre

Setting (Time & Place)

Main Cast

Supporting Cast

Plot

MY MOVIE LOGBOOK

My Review

_____

_____

_____

_____

_____

_____

_____

_____

_____

_____

Extra Notes

_____

_____

_____

_____

Rating: ☆☆☆☆☆

MY MOVIE LOGBOOK

Movie Title

Director

Genre

Setting (Time & Place)

Main Cast

Supporting Cast

Plot

MY MOVIE LOGBOOK

My Review

Extra Notes

Rating: ☆☆☆☆☆

MY MOVIE LOGBOOK

Movie Title

Director

Genre

Setting (Time & Place)

Main Cast

Supporting Cast

Plot

MY MOVIE LOGBOOK

My Review

_____
_____
_____
_____
_____
_____
_____
_____
_____
_____

Extra Notes

_____
_____
_____

Rating: ☆☆☆☆☆

MY MOVIE LOGBOOK

Movie Title

Director

Genre

Setting (Time & Place)

Main Cast

Supporting Cast

Plot

MY MOVIE LOGBOOK

My Review

Extra Notes

Rating: ☆☆☆☆☆

MY MOVIE LOGBOOK

Movie Title

Director

Genre

Setting (Time & Place)

Main Cast

Supporting Cast

Plot

MY MOVIE LOGBOOK

My Review

_____

_____

_____

_____

_____

_____

_____

_____

_____

_____

Extra Notes

_____

_____

_____

Rating: ☆☆☆☆☆

MY MOVIE LOGBOOK

Movie Title

Director

Genre

Setting (Time & Place)

Main Cast

Supporting Cast

Plot

MY MOVIE LOGBOOK

My Review

_____

_____

_____

_____

_____

_____

_____

_____

_____

_____

_____

Extra Notes

_____

_____

_____

Rating: ☆☆☆☆☆

MY MOVIE LOGBOOK

Movie Title

Director

Genre

Setting (Time & Place)

Main Cast

Supporting Cast

Plot

MY MOVIE LOGBOOK

My Review

_____

_____

_____

_____

_____

_____

_____

_____

_____

Extra Notes

_____

_____

_____

Rating: ☆☆☆☆☆

MY MOVIE LOGBOOK

Movie Title

Director

Genre

Setting (Time & Place)

Main Cast

Supporting Cast

Plot

MY MOVIE LOGBOOK

My Review

Extra Notes

Rating: ☆☆☆☆☆

MY MOVIE LOGBOOK

Movie Title

Director

Genre

Setting (Time & Place)

Main Cast

Supporting Cast

Plot

MY MOVIE LOGBOOK

My Review

Extra Notes

Rating: ☆☆☆☆☆

MY MOVIE LOGBOOK

Movie Title

Director

Genre

Setting (Time & Place)

Main Cast

Supporting Cast

Plot

MY MOVIE LOGBOOK

My Review

Extra Notes

Rating: ☆☆☆☆☆

MY MOVIE LOGBOOK

Movie Title

Director

Genre

Setting (Time & Place)

Main Cast

Supporting Cast

Plot

MY MOVIE LOGBOOK

My Review

_____

_____

_____

_____

_____

_____

_____

_____

_____

Extra Notes

_____

_____

_____

Rating: ☆☆☆☆☆

MY MOVIE LOGBOOK

Movie Title

Director

Genre

Setting (Time & Place)

Main Cast

Supporting Cast

Plot

MY MOVIE LOGBOOK

My Review

Extra Notes

Rating: ☆☆☆☆☆

MY MOVIE LOGBOOK

Movie Title

Director

Genre

Setting (Time & Place)

Main Cast

Supporting Cast

Plot

MY MOVIE LOGBOOK

My Review

_____

_____

_____

_____

_____

_____

_____

_____

_____

_____

_____

Extra Notes

_____

_____

_____

Rating: ☆☆☆☆☆

MY MOVIE LOGBOOK

Movie Title

Director

Genre

Setting (Time & Place)

Main Cast

Supporting Cast

Plot

MY MOVIE LOGBOOK

My Review

Extra Notes

Rating:

MY MOVIE LOGBOOK

Movie Title

Director

Genre

Setting (Time & Place)

Main Cast

Supporting Cast

Plot

MY MOVIE LOGBOOK

My Review

_____

_____

_____

_____

_____

_____

_____

_____

_____

_____

Extra Notes

_____

_____

_____

Rating: ☆☆☆☆☆

MY MOVIE LOGBOOK

Movie Title

Director

Genre

Setting (Time & Place)

Main Cast

Supporting Cast

Plot

MY MOVIE LOGBOOK

My Review

_____

_____

_____

_____

_____

_____

_____

_____

_____

Extra Notes

_____

_____

_____

Rating: ☆☆☆☆☆

MY MOVIE LOGBOOK

Movie Title

Director

Genre

Setting (Time & Place)

Main Cast

Supporting Cast

Plot

MY MOVIE LOGBOOK

My Review

_____

_____

_____

_____

_____

_____

_____

_____

_____

_____

Extra Notes

_____

_____

_____

Rating: ☆☆☆☆☆

MY MOVIE LOGBOOK

Movie Title

Director

Genre

Setting (Time & Place)

Main Cast

Supporting Cast

Plot

MY MOVIE LOGBOOK

My Review

_____

_____

_____

_____

_____

_____

_____

_____

Extra Notes

_____

_____

_____

Rating: ☆☆☆☆☆

MY MOVIE LOGBOOK

Movie Title

Director

Genre

Setting (Time & Place)

Main Cast

Supporting Cast

Plot

MY MOVIE LOGBOOK

My Review

Extra Notes

Rating: ☆☆☆☆☆

MY MOVIE LOGBOOK

Movie Title

Director

Genre

Setting (Time & Place)

Main Cast

Supporting Cast

Plot

MY MOVIE LOGBOOK

My Review

_____

_____

_____

_____

_____

_____

_____

_____

Extra Notes

_____

_____

_____

Rating: ☆☆☆☆☆

MY MOVIE LOGBOOK

Movie Title

Director

Genre

Setting (Time & Place)

Main Cast

Supporting Cast

Plot

MY MOVIE LOGBOOK

My Review

_____

_____

_____

_____

_____

_____

_____

_____

_____

Extra Notes

_____

_____

_____

_____

Rating: ☆ ☆ ☆ ☆ ☆

MY MOVIE LOGBOOK

Movie Title

Director

Genre

Setting (Time & Place)

Main Cast

Supporting Cast

Plot

MY MOVIE LOGBOOK

My Review

_____

_____

_____

_____

_____

_____

_____

_____

_____

Extra Notes

_____

_____

_____

Rating: ☆☆☆☆☆

MY MOVIE LOGBOOK

Movie Title

Director

Genre

Setting (Time & Place)

Main Cast

Supporting Cast

Plot

MY MOVIE LOGBOOK

My Review

Extra Notes

Rating: ☆☆☆☆☆

MY MOVIE LOGBOOK

Movie Title
_____

Director
_____

Genre
_____

Setting (Time & Place)
_____

_____

Main Cast
_____

_____

_____

Supporting Cast
_____

_____

Plot
_____

_____

_____

_____

_____

_____

_____

MY MOVIE LOGBOOK

My Review

_____

_____

_____

_____

_____

_____

_____

_____

Extra Notes

_____

_____

_____

Rating: ☆☆☆☆☆

MY MOVIE LOGBOOK

Movie Title

Director

Genre

Setting (Time & Place)

Main Cast

Supporting Cast

Plot

MY MOVIE LOGBOOK

My Review

_____

_____

_____

_____

_____

_____

_____

_____

_____

_____

Extra Notes

_____

_____

_____

Rating: ☆☆☆☆☆

MY MOVIE LOGBOOK

Movie Title

Director

Genre

Setting (Time & Place)

Main Cast

Supporting Cast

Plot

MY MOVIE LOGBOOK

My Review

_____

_____

_____

_____

_____

_____

_____

_____

_____

_____

Extra Notes

_____

_____

_____

Rating: ☆ ☆ ☆ ☆ ☆

MY MOVIE LOGBOOK

Movie Title

Director

Genre

Setting (Time & Place)

Main Cast

Supporting Cast

Plot

MY MOVIE LOGBOOK

My Review

_____

_____

_____

_____

_____

_____

_____

_____

_____

Extra Notes

_____

_____

_____

Rating: ☆☆☆☆☆

MY MOVIE LOGBOOK

Movie Title

Director

Genre

Setting (Time & Place)

Main Cast

Supporting Cast

Plot

MY MOVIE LOGBOOK

My Review

_____

_____

_____

_____

_____

_____

_____

_____

Extra Notes

_____

_____

_____

Rating: ☆☆☆☆☆

MY MOVIE LOGBOOK

Movie Title

Director

Genre

Setting (Time & Place)

Main Cast

Supporting Cast

Plot

MY MOVIE LOGBOOK

My Review

_____

_____

_____

_____

_____

_____

_____

_____

_____

Extra Notes

_____

_____

_____

Rating: ☆☆☆☆☆

MY MOVIE LOGBOOK

Movie Title

Director

Genre

Setting (Time & Place)

Main Cast

Supporting Cast

Plot

MY MOVIE LOGBOOK

My Review

Extra Notes

Rating: ☆☆☆☆☆

MY MOVIE LOGBOOK

Movie Title

Director

Genre

Setting (Time & Place)

Main Cast

Supporting Cast

Plot

MY MOVIE LOGBOOK

My Review

_____

_____

_____

_____

_____

_____

_____

_____

_____

_____

Extra Notes

_____

_____

_____

Rating: ☆☆☆☆☆

MY MOVIE LOGBOOK

Movie Title

Director

Genre

Setting (Time & Place)

Main Cast

Supporting Cast

Plot

MY MOVIE LOGBOOK

My Review

Extra Notes

Rating: ☆☆☆☆☆

MY MOVIE LOGBOOK

Movie Title

Director

Genre

Setting (Time & Place)

Main Cast

Supporting Cast

Plot

MY MOVIE LOGBOOK

My Review

_____

_____

_____

_____

_____

_____

_____

_____

_____

_____

Extra Notes

_____

_____

_____

Rating: ☆ ☆ ☆ ☆ ☆

MY MOVIE LOGBOOK

Movie Title

Director

Genre

Setting (Time & Place)

Main Cast

Supporting Cast

Plot

MY MOVIE LOGBOOK

My Review

_____
_____
_____
_____
_____
_____
_____
_____
_____

Extra Notes

_____
_____
_____

Rating: ☆☆☆☆☆

MY MOVIE LOGBOOK

Movie Title

Director

Genre

Setting (Time & Place)

Main Cast

Supporting Cast

Plot

MY MOVIE LOGBOOK

My Review

_____

_____

_____

_____

_____

_____

_____

_____

_____

_____

Extra Notes

_____

_____

_____

_____

Rating: ☆☆☆☆☆

MY MOVIE LOGBOOK

Movie Title
_____

Director
_____

Genre
_____

Setting (Time & Place)
_____
_____

Main Cast
_____
_____
_____

Supporting Cast
_____
_____

Plot
_____
_____
_____
_____
_____
_____
_____

MY MOVIE LOGBOOK

My Review

Extra Notes

Rating: ☆☆☆☆☆

MY MOVIE LOGBOOK

Movie Title
_____

Director
_____

Genre
_____

Setting (Time & Place)
_____
_____

Main Cast
_____
_____
_____

Supporting Cast
_____
_____

Plot
_____
_____
_____
_____
_____
_____
_____

MY MOVIE LOGBOOK

My Review

_____

_____

_____

_____

_____

_____

_____

_____

_____

_____

Extra Notes

_____

_____

_____

Rating: ☆☆☆☆☆

MY MOVIE LOGBOOK

Movie Title

Director

Genre

Setting (Time & Place)

Main Cast

Supporting Cast

Plot

MY MOVIE LOGBOOK

My Review

Extra Notes

Rating: ☆☆☆☆☆

MY MOVIE LOGBOOK

Movie Title

Director

Genre

Setting (Time & Place)

Main Cast

Supporting Cast

Plot

MY MOVIE LOGBOOK

My Review

_____

_____

_____

_____

_____

_____

_____

_____

_____

_____

Extra Notes

_____

_____

_____

Rating: ☆☆☆☆☆

MY MOVIE LOGBOOK

Movie Title

Director

Genre

Setting (Time & Place)

Main Cast

Supporting Cast

Plot

MY MOVIE LOGBOOK

My Review

_____

_____

_____

_____

_____

_____

_____

_____

_____

_____

Extra Notes

_____

_____

_____

_____

Rating: ☆☆☆☆☆

MY MOVIE LOGBOOK

Movie Title

Director

Genre

Setting (Time & Place)

Main Cast

Supporting Cast

Plot

MY MOVIE LOGBOOK

My Review

_____

_____

_____

_____

_____

_____

_____

_____

Extra Notes

_____

_____

_____

Rating: ☆☆☆☆☆

Printed in Great Britain
by Amazon

74822504R00059